Oldh
Inspirational Library
Volume 1

How to Grow Spiritually

By W. Dale Oldham

Large-Print
Abridged Edition

Warner Press

Anderson, Indiana

Coordinator of Communications and Publishing
Church of God Ministries, Inc.
PO Box 2420, Anderson, IN 46018-2420
800-848-2464 • www.chog.org

To purchase additional copies of this book, to inquire about distribution and for all other sales-related matters, please contact:

Warner Press, Inc.
PO Box 2499, Anderson, IN 46018-9988
877-346-3974 • www.warnerpress.com

Text abridgement: Joseph D. Allison
Cover design: Carolyn A. Frost
ISBN 978-1-59317-178-0

Library of Congress Cataloging-in-Publication Data

Oldham, Dale.
    [Just across the street]
    How to grow spiritually / by W. Dale Oldham. -- Abridged large-print ed.
        p.   cm. -- (Oldham inspirational library ; v. 1)
    Originally published: Just across the street. Anderson, Ind. : Warner Press, 1968.
    ISBN 978-1-59317-178-0 (pbk.)
    1. Christian life. 2. Large type books. I. Title.
    BV4501.3.O458 2007
    248.4--dc22   2007017036

Printed in the United States of America
07 08 09 10 11 / EP / 10 9 8 7 6 5 4 3 2 1

Table of Contents

To Polly,
without whose steadying love
these pages would not
have been written.

Publisher's Preface

In the foreword to the first edition, Dale Oldham noted that every Christian realizes the need for spiritual growth. He wrote:

> ...Since our conversion, we have experienced certain disillusionments. Back there we naively thought that conversion would solve all our problems, prefect all our personal relationships. Now we know that conversion was but a door opening into vast and wonderful possibilities and in our relationships with people...

> This book is an attempt to help us understand ourselves better, for many times to understand is to open another door to growth...

Though Dr. Oldham did not claim to be a psychiatrist, he had remarkable insight into the human psyche as well as the soul. In this book, he highlights a variety of emotional and spiritual problems that can impede a Christian's growth. He offers the counsel of God's Word in dealing with them.

We have abridged and updated the book to make it more accessible to today's busy reader. We commend it to you as a practical guide for your own daily discipleship.

1. What Do You Think of Yourself?

All of us desire to grow spiritually, but it is impossible for us to move forward until we glimpse two pictures of ourselves: a picture of what we are right now and a vision of what we can become by the grace of a loving God.

What you think of yourself — what you believe to be true concerning your character, your ambitions, your unrealized potentials — is of tremendous importance. Your opinion of yourself stays with you, not only consciously, but subconsciously. Everything you do or attempt to do or refuse to do reflects that self-image.

Perhaps the pastor asks you to accept a certain responsibility in the church, but you reply, "Oh, I couldn't possibly handle that kind of an assignment." This is your self-image. This is what you think of your abilities, what you think to be true about yourself. And when you believe a thing to be true, your belief helps to make it come true. Whoever has been known to transcend his dreams?

While I was in college, a fellow student became angry with the president of the school. One midnight, he packed up and left, never to return. Elsewhere he finished his college work, took a graduate degree, then entered the field of secondary education, where he did well, soon becoming principal of a high school. But the work proved too routine for his restless, ambitious nature.

One day he wrote a letter to Charles F. Kettering, who at the time was head of research and sales for General Motors, telling Mr. Kettering he desired to work for him. There was no reply. He wrote a second letter, saying about the same thing, but again there was no answer. Irritated but not abashed, my friend went to Detroit, located the General Motors office building, took an elevator to the floor of Mr. Kettering's office, and found himself in a reception room facing Mr. Kettering's secretary.

"Is that Mr. Kettering's office?" he asked, pointing to a door. When the girl nodded, my friend, without asking permission, walked past her right into Mr. Kettering's office. The surprised executive looked up and fumed, "Well! You've got your nerve! Who are you and what do you want?"

With a disarming smile, my friend replied, "It's like this, Mr. Kettering. I wrote you twice asking for a job, but you didn't even reply. I thought I'd come up here to see just what kind of a man you are. But before you say anything else, I think I ought to tell you that I've made up my mind I'm going to work for you, so you may as well give me a job."

His audacity brought a smile to Kettering, who asked, "What can you do?"

"I don't know," my friend replied, "I'm raw material." He got a job with General Motors, and it was a good one. Before long, he was flying back and forth across the country, addressing large groups of sales people on the merits of Chevrolets and Frigidaires. But he would never have made an effort toward advancement had he not caught an image of what he could become.

Another friend of mine was offered promotion to a management job but turned it down, saying, "I don't think I could handle that kind of responsibility." His boss was sure he could or he never would have made the offer, but he turned it down. Through the intervening years, he has continued to work at the lesser job with its ordinary salary, just because of the inferior quality of his self-image.

Your self-image is very important in everything you do. What you think of yourself will condition your emotions, your activities, your ambitions. It will limit or liberate your abilities.

Do you remember the Old Testament story about Gideon? The angel of the Lord told Gideon that God wanted him to lead his people to victory, to liberate them from the heavy hand of oppression. Gideon, with no faith at all in his leadership abilities, said, "The Lord has cast us off" (Judg 6:13). His self-image was that of a forsaken, doomed man living among helpless, defeated people. He said, "My clan is the weakest in Manasseh, and I am the least in my family" (v. 15). But the Lord didn't give up, for he knew things about Gideon that Gideon didn't know about himself. Only after the Lord allowed some things to happen that partially cured Gideon of his paralyzing feeling of inferiority did he begin to hope and then to believe.

Finally, we read, "the spirit of the Lord took possession of Gideon; and he sounded the trumpet" (v. 34), making public his acceptance of the divine assignment. To his surprise and gratification, men began rallying around him from all directions. Judges 7 tells how, with his self-image completely redeemed, Gideon led his people to a smashing victory. They were once again free.

Moses had a similar experience when God called him to lead the Hebrews out of Egyptian bondage (see Ex 4). Isaiah experienced a similar change in attitude (see Isa 6).

If you think you are a failure, you will fail; but if through faith in God's power you believe you can succeed, you will. Second Corinthians 3:18 says, "All of us who are Christians ..., reflect like mirrors the glory of the Lord. We are transfigured by the Spirit of the Lord in ever-increasing splendor into his own image" (Phillips). Is this a failure image? No, it is a success image to the nth degree. Our new image of ourselves as Christians will mirror the glory of God. There will be an "ever-increasing splendor" about it. The new self-image becomes a combination of what Christ can do for us, what we believe, and what we do for ourselves.

2. You Can Change!

Are you satisfied with the progress you have made as a Christian, or have you lost ground? Have you found happiness in the Lord, or is there a nagging desire to be different?

Jesus said, "Blessed are those who hunger and thirst for righteousness, for they will be filled" (Matt 5:6). Hunger and thirst are driving desires. Do you hunger and thirst after righteousness? No change will come in your life or in your relationship to Christ unless you crave that change with your whole heart. God means business with us; we must mean business with him.

Paul said that you can be renewed "in the spirit of your mind." He said that you can put on a new nature, created after the likeness of God "in true righteousness and holiness" (Eph 4:23–24). Invariably, we apply these verses to the unconverted, but we need to remember that originally they were written to Christians. They were addressed "to the saints who are in Ephesus and are faithful in Christ Jesus" (1:1). If Paul wrote like that to Christians, why should we not expect nominally Christian people to find renewal, rehabilitation, and transformation through recommitment, a deepening of their love, and a clarification of their vision? I've seen it happen again and again. It has happened to prominent church workers, teachers, trustees, even preachers who for years had been telling other folk how to live.

I remember a nationally known minister who used to come periodically to lecture at the seminary I attended in Dayton, Ohio. He had gained prominence, popularity, and wide acclaim, and was pastor of a church with several thousand members. But for some reason, I did not like the man. He was too self-assured, suave, and smooth. To my way of thinking, his whole manner exuded a sophisticated air of worldliness that was at a distinct variance with the spirit of

Christ. He seemed to enjoy shocking audiences with overly frank statements and illustrations. So, after hearing him a time or two, I avoided his lectures and was not enthusiastic about reading his books.

Years later, during my pastorate at Park Place Church in Anderson, this same man was invited to lecture at Anderson College. The college asked me to invite him to our church on prayer meeting night and then contribute toward his expenses. You will understand my reluctance in doing this, but finally I relented. The speaker came, delivered a most excellent address and, to my happy surprise, exhibited a most humble, lovable, charming Christian spirit. Actually, he was so changed that immediately after the benediction, I turned, took his hand, and with a smile asked, "When did it happen?"

He knew exactly what I meant and answered, "Four or five years ago. I'll tell you about it while I am here." And he did.

Here was a brilliant man who had experienced a radical change of heart and personality in his fifties, after having been a preacher of the gospel for more than thirty years. Most of his friends would agree that his last ten years were the most wholesome and fruitful of his entire career. He had indeed "put off" his old nature and "put on" a new nature, created after the likeness of God, in true righteousness and holiness. Salvation in Christ had become for him a well of living water, springing up into everlasting life.

A certain businessman had been brought up in the church, had made a commitment to Christ and been baptized in his teens, and had been involved in church work in one way or another all his life. Somewhere along the line, Christ lost priority in this man's experience. In spite of this, at about the age of fifty, my friend made a fresh commitment to Christ. Watching the miracle of his change, I was reminded of the words Christ spoke to his disciples concerning the

Holy Spirit: "He abides with you, and he will be in you" (John 14:17). Does this need to happen to you?

Several years ago, a woman of perhaps forty wrote to pour out some of her problems and difficulties with the hope that I could be of some help to her. Her husband was an alcoholic, and she had carried the burden so long that it was about to get her down. The load was simply too much for her to bear. I answered her letter, and later she made a trip to Anderson for counseling. We had a long talk together, and I truly felt sorry for her. Finally, she said in some desperation, "What can I do?" Divorce offered a way out, but she had deep religious convictions against divorce, feeling that even if justified, it would be followed in her heart by a disastrous sense of failure.

I outlined for her a program of spiritual disciplines and reading that I thought might help her to rise above her problems. We prayed and she returned home. Months later, I had a letter from her in which she said,

"Thank you for your help and guidance. The Lord is hearing and answering prayer, but not in the way I had thought it might happen. Recently, I have found that peace can be mine, not through the removal of my problems, but in spite of them. My husband hasn't changed a bit, but I have. And I have found in a closer walk with God the ability to face the present and the future without fear and without any sense of defeat."

This woman had placed her life, together with all her problems, squarely in the capable hands of Christ. As the old song has it, she could say, "When He lifts my burdens, He lifts me, too."

Another friend of mine has come into his best years since his seventy-fifth birthday. I think that is a real miracle. After seventy-five, he has experienced a spiritual rebirth. He is growing old sweetly, graciously, and with a lovable Christian spirit. So it can happen to anyone for whom it becomes the foremost desire of the heart.

It is simply amazing what the grace of God can do by way of changing Christian people, but you don't change until you clearly see your need to change. Like the Prodigal, you must first come to yourself. The satisfied person never does anything to promote spiritual growth, and the self-righteous person is blind even to the need to grow. But for those who hunger and thirst after righteousness, growth and spiritual transformation are possible at any age.

---

3. Break the Barrier

I remember a visit to Daytona Beach, that intriguing stretch of seashore where you can drive your automobile for seventeen miles on sand almost as hard as pavement. This beach was once made famous by the automobile races held there. Standing there, watching the waves meet the shore, it is natural to think of eternity.

As far as the eye can see, there is water; it seems to extend to the ends of the earth.

The waves roll in unceasingly, just as you know they are rolling in on a thousand beaches around the world. The water is never really quiet. Year after year, the waves roll in, night and day. Tides rise and fall; calm and storm succeed each other. But the inward rush of water is always stopped by the rising angle of the land. The sandy shore remains a barrier, as century follows century and time is pushed onward toward eternity.

I remember visiting another beach on the troubled Outer Banks of North Carolina that lead south toward Cape Hatteras. This stretch of shore is so boisterous and treacherous that it has been aptly called a graveyard of ships. But even in this turbulent area, the sand is a barrier to the ocean. The boiling waves sweep up and up, as if they would conquer every inch of the stubbornly resisting land. They deposit their flecked foam high but come to a reluctant stop and slip back into the sea which gave them birth.

Not always are the waves held in check. A few times in North Carolina's history, the Outer Banks have failed to hold back the raging sea. Towering tidal waves, caused by a hurricane or some underwater upheaval of the earth, have come crashing across the beach, carrying everything before them, until finally they lost their force in Kittyhawk Bay and other inside coastal waterways of the Tar Heel state. Natives tell stories of houses that were smashed into splinters by the uncontrolled power of the waves, of boats, large and small, that were destroyed as the raging sea leaped its barriers in a desperate search for freedom.

Waves crashing on the beach are an analogy to the questing spirit of mankind. Why do some people seem never able to muster up the courage to challenge the barriers encircling them? So many kinds of barriers hold people back: greed, guilt, doubt, laziness, pride. For some, hatred and hostility build a wall that is both high and impenetrable. Some of these barriers seem to thicken and grow with the passing years.

But history is replete with thrilling stories of those who were not content to remain prisoners of circumstances. They broke the barriers of their lives and escaped to new life, while others seemed unaware that escape was either possible or desirable.

When wickedness was everywhere, a man named Noah broke through the tangled maze to find fellowship with God. "But Noah found favor in the sight of the Lord," we read in Genesis 6:8. The Lord said to Noah, "Go into the ark, you and all your household, for I have seen that you are righteous before me in this generation" (7:1).

Musing upon this event long centuries afterward, a New Testament writer recorded in Hebrews 11:7, "By faith Noah, warned by God about events as yet unseen, respected the warning and built an ark to save his household; by this he condemned the world and became an heir to the righteousness that is in accordance with faith." Noah broke the barrier. He dared to be different in his faith, in his attitude toward God, and in his day-by-day conduct.

While still a young man, Abram broke through a barrier that had for centuries kept everyone about him from discovering and worshiping the one true God. In Ur of the Chaldees, where in former days rebellious men had built the Tower of Babel, Abram became conscious of something different, something better. So while his neighbors, friends, and relatives proceeded with their ignorant, idolatrous ways, Abram brooded concerning God, his will, and his way.

Abram broke forth into the freedom known only to those who irrevocably take their stand for God. He dared to trust the guidance of his heart, dared to be different, dared to stand for the truth, even when it meant standing alone. So we read in Genesis 12:1, "Now the Lord said to Abram, 'Go from your country and your kindred and your father's house to the land that I will show you.'" So Abram went out, not knowing where he was being led, but following the voice of God. Thus, in one great leap of obedience and trusting faith, he broke the barrier of paganism and idolatry to find new life and blessing in God. He was not content to maintain the status quo or to remain contained by barriers. We bless him for his faith and courage.

There are so many barriers to the abundant life, so many hindrances to a vital relationship with God and Christ and the Holy Spirit. The age in which we live does not make it easier for us to serve the Lord. Yet invariably, barriers go crashing down when we align our lives to the will of God and submit ourselves to the law of love.

4. You Are What You Believe

A man said to me, "It doesn't make any difference what a person be-lieves as long as he is sincere." That may have sounded like a very broad-minded statement to him, but to me it was just plain nonsense.

What we believe makes the difference between life and death, peace and pain, hope and despair, trust and pessimism, heaven and hell. I may hand you a bottle labeled "Essence of Peppermint" when ac-tually it contains deadly strychnine. If you drink the contents, you will die, no matter what you believe the bottle contains. It is tremendously important that we believe the truth. Nothing erects a barrier to personal growth more quickly than to believe a lie.

E. Griffith Jones insists that "all of us in the end tend to become what we are in virtue of the operative beliefs of our life." Give that statement a great deal of careful thought. The "operative beliefs of his life" sent Jesus to the cross, sent Stephen to a martyr's death, sent Demas back to Thessalonica, and Judas Iscariot to self-destruction. So don't think for a moment that it makes little difference what you believe or if you believe.

Just what do you believe? What are your convictions? What do you accept as being true? The answers will make a tremendous difference in the way you live, the way you handle your job, the way you get along with people, the quality of your family life, and your attitude toward the future. Benedict Arnold was the product of what he believed. So was Abraham Lincoln. So are you. What you believe makes a difference in the way you live and the way you die.

Ancient Romans were impressed by the tranquility and courage of Christian martyrs who unflinchingly laid down their lives out of love for their Master. The second-century Christian writer Tertullian explained, "No man would be willing to thus die unless he knew he had the truth."[1]

Faith is established by what a person believes! What do you believe about Christ, redemption, the church, the Holy Spirit, Christian unity, the end of the world? The quality of your life and the nature of your final destiny are all wrapped up in what you believe.

Perhaps you have read the story of George Matheson, who began his ministry with a serious lack of faith in God and a big question in his mind about immortality. He was not even sure that we humans possess souls. (One wonders why he ever entered the ministry with such misgivings!) But because he was honest in his doubting and possessed an earnestly seeking heart, the Lord led him one step at a time to solid ground. Some years later, his eyesight began to fail. When he sadly shared the fact of his coming blindness with the

---

1. John Sutherland Bonnell, *What Are You Living For?* (Nashville, TN: Abingdon-Cokesbury Press, 1950), 20.

young woman to whom he was engaged, she broke their agreement and left him.

George Matheson did go blind. What a testing time for his faith! Yet out of that crucible of sadness, disappointment, and trial, Matheson wrote these words:

> O Love, that wilt not let me go,
> I rest my weary soul in Thee;
> I give Thee back the life I owe,
> That in Thine ocean depths, its flow
> May richer, fuller be.
>
> O Joy, that seekest me through pain,
> I cannot close my heart to Thee;
> I trace the rainbow through the rain,
> And feel the promise is not vain,
> That morn shall tearless be.

This is how a genuine faith in God supports us when troubles come. And who knows when tragedy will strike? Who knows what the future holds? Will our faith, our belief, our trust in God be strong enough to provide for us a harbor in the storm? Do we believe enough to be held safe and secure when the tempest is raging? It is high time for you and me to take inventory.

I walked into Dr. Carl Kardatzke's room shortly after his doctor had told him he had but three months to live. He and his wife were talking as I entered. He said, "We have just been thanking God for the privilege of serving him down through the years. We have had such unusual opportunities to serve people. We have been thanking him for our Christian children and the wonderful family life we have enjoyed together. God has been very good to us."

In following visits, I never failed to find my friend sustained by an unfaltering faith in God. Now and then he would say, "Pastor, you are always praying for me. Today I want to offer the prayer." I would leave his presence feeling that a benediction had been pronounced upon me.

You see, we die as we live. Live in the faith and you need not worry about how you will die.

---

5. Is Your Conversion Incomplete?

A certain man was an alcoholic, and his alcoholism was ruining his career, his marriage, and his family life. His children were humiliated by their father's deteriorating reputation in the community; his wife spent a great deal of time praying and weeping over his condition. Neighbors for the most part were sympathetic. They pitied the wife and children as much as they did the man. This unfortunate fellow was likable, but weak. Increasingly, there built up within him a desire to quit his drinking and regain the respectability he had lost. So one day, through prayer and a strong desire to be free, he managed to quit his drinking, once and for all. The habit was broken. His wife and children were overjoyed, feeling they had been given a new husband and father. A fresh, new happiness came into the home.

Nearby, in the little church the family attended, this changed man was invited to give his testimony. Everyone rejoiced in his newfound victory. The days of his drinking were over, and with this change he found a new circle of friends within the church. Not that he had been soundly converted. Apparently, the drinking habit had been broken, but nothing else changed about him; only his alcoholism was gone. The other bad habits and attitudes, the old vocabulary, remained.

So here was a man partly converted, partially changed and made new. He was blind to the fact that his change had been but partial. Since drinking had been his worst and most obvious bad habit, he seemed to assume that he had experienced a new birth in Christ. But this was not the case; he had only quit drinking.

A short time after this, I became his pastor. I tried to tactfully suggest to him that he had not been thoroughly converted and that this was still his greatest need. This offended him and he stayed away from church for a few months. Finally, however, he confessed his further need and made a full commitment to Christ. Afterward, he said, "Thank you, Pastor, for being true to my soul. Had you permitted me to go on as I was, I might have died without ever having cleared my soul before God."

Perhaps most people experience a clean conversion when they come to Christ. Old things pass away and all things become new (see 2 Cor 5:17). But there are others for whom this simply doesn't happen, generally because they are unwilling to do what is necessary for it to happen.

Some new Christians accept God's forgiveness of sin, but no real regeneration of personality is evident. They bog down under the weight of personality defects that others feel should have been brought to happy resolution by the grace of God. They are like those to whom the writer of Hebrews said, "You have been Christians a long time now, and you ought to be teaching others. Instead, you need someone to teach you again the basic things a beginner must learn about the Scriptures." Then he added, "Solid food is for those who are mature, who have trained themselves to recognize the difference between right and wrong and then do what is right" (Heb 5:12, 14 NLT).

Do you suppose that many Christians have been but partially converted? This may explain why they are confused; they have not experienced a more complete spiritual renovation.

One pastor, in whose church there was a flaming race prejudice, said, "It is my feeling that we are converted in different areas at different times in our lives. Many of my parishioners are simply not yet converted to Christ's view of brotherhood. But I do not question their conversion at other levels." Yet Paul wrote in Romans 8:9, "Anyone who does not have the Spirit of Christ does not belong to him." The Lord can take from us only what we freely offer up to him. We receive according to the quality and completeness of our love and our surrender. If we hold back anything, then certain areas of spiritual victory will be held back from us, for Christ can convert only those areas of our personality that are placed under his full control.

I want to be sure about my relationship to Christ, don't you? I don't want to be a halfway Christian. This means a complete transference of sovereignty from self to God. It means being so filled with the Spirit of Christ that we can say with Paul, "It is no longer I who live, but it is Christ who lives in me" (Gal 2:20). There is no joy in an experience of partial conversion. Some Christians have little victory because they have never surrendered their money to God's control. Others have not submitted their desires to him, or their affections.

It is so easy these days to be tinged with Christianity, influenced by the church, changed to some degree by prayer, without being transformed by repentance, forgiveness, and the new birth. One wonders how many Christians have actually stopped with Old Testament religion. In Old Testament times, God's people found forgiveness without regeneration. But for us, forgiveness without regeneration means weakness and ineffectiveness in the Christian life. Jesus said, "You must be born again" (John 3:7 NLT). All the way.

6. How to Handle Guilt Feelings

We say we want to grow spiritually but fail to grow as we should; we are apt to alibi for ourselves or blame our failure on someone else. This is where we often get ourselves into long-lasting trouble of a serious nature. It's like this: when we do wrong, we send an arrow of guilt deep into our hearts, and it affects both the conscious and the subconscious mind.

Years ago, a friend of mine gave his heart to the Lord and was genuinely converted. He then was faced with quite a problem. Over a period of several years, he had stolen one tool after another from the company where he worked. In fact, one whole wall of his garage was hung with the tools he had taken. In addition, he had smuggled out of the shop some sixty-four gallons of highly refined oil, one quart at a time, in his dinner bucket. No Christian conscience should ever be at peace in such a situation, for the Bible plainly says, "Take it back." (See Ezek 33:15.)

My friend really meant business in serving the Lord, so he knew the day of restitution had to be faced, and soon. It was the month of December; he waited until

Christmas morning and then knocked at the door of the plant superintendent, who answered in person. Not a man to waste time, my friend said, "I just got saved." (That was the way his own pastor would have said it.)

He continued, "I've been going to a revival meeting down at the church and got under conviction. So I went down there with some of the others and prayed. I told God I was sorry and that if he would forgive me, I'd straighten things out and serve him the rest of my life. Now, I've got a problem. During the years I've been working for you, I've been taking tools that didn't belong to me. In fact, the whole side of my garage is hung full of them."

There was a long silence — too long for my confessing friend, who could not tell by the expression on the superintendent's face just what he was thinking. When no response was forthcoming, my friend blurted, "What shall I do with the tools?"

The superintendent answered, "Take them back where you got them."

"What are you going to do with me?"

There was another long pause. Then, with a bit of humor lighting up his eyes, the boss replied, "I'm going to pray that the kind of religion you've found will spread throughout the plant. If it does, there will be truckloads of tools coming back along with yours."

No wonder my friend was such a happy Christian down through the years until the Lord called him home. When he gave his heart to the Lord, he came all the way; he cleaned house.

A very wise person wrote many centuries ago, "No one who conceals transgressions will prosper" (Prov 28:13a). If we do not face up to them, these repressed, covered feelings of guilt can cause all kinds of trouble — irritability, nervousness, sleeplessness, indigestion, worry, fear, loss of interest in home and work. In spite of this, many people will do almost anything in the world except confess that they have done wrong and ask forgiveness for it.

Guilt for sin cannot be removed from the heart by some magic formula, ritual, or ceremony; it can be dealt with only by the Lord himself. You can weep and pray, but if your attitude is not one of genuine repentance and sorrow for sin, relief will not come. You can counsel with a psychiatrist, who may be able to help you reduce your feelings of guilt, but only God can forgive sin and lift that burden of condemnation from your heart. Your sin must be confessed. It has to be brought out into the open and dealt with.

John wrote, "If we confess our sins, he who is faithful and just will forgive us our sins and cleanse us from all unrighteousness" (1 John 1:9). To gloss over our sins and refuse to acknowledge that we have sinned will only increase what may eventually become an untenable burden of guilt.

Take a look at the rest of that verse from Proverbs: "No one who conceals transgressions will prosper, but one who confesses and forsakes them will obtain mercy" (Prov 28:13). This is exactly the way it works out. When you conceal your sin, it turns into guilt; but when you confess and forsake it, you clear the way for spiritual healing and happiness.

Heartfelt repentance is good medicine for the soul. It promotes peace of mind and a sense of fellowship with God. The burden is lifted. Now you can pray with assurance.

---

7. Resentment Is Your Enemy

The development of a mature Christian personality is a lifetime job. It calls for adding some things to our experience and keeping others out. Resentment is one spiritually debilitating attitude that should be locked out. Resentment has destroyed the spiritual vitality and joy of thousands of Christians.

Judas Iscariot learned this the hard way. You remember the supper that Jesus attended in the home of Mary, Martha, and Lazarus. After supper, Mary poured a very costly bottle of perfume over the feet of Jesus; then she wiped them with her hair. Commentators say the perfume was worth about sixty dollars in American money. Did you ever own a sixty-dollar bottle of perfume? What a luxury! To Judas's way of thinking, the money was absolutely wasted. Who ever heard of perfume being poured on a man's feet? Besides, she had poured no perfume on Judas's feet. So here was resentment, mixed with greed and a bit of jealousy, gnawing away at the soul of Judas.

Resentment is your enemy! Learn to recognize its earliest appearance.

A young mother came to me one day, overflowing with resentment. She said her four young children were simply too demanding. They took too much of her time and were tying her down. In fact, she said tearfully, she was a virtual slave to her family. She couldn't come and go as she desired, for she was chained to such humdrum chores as cooking, doing the dishes, making beds, and taking care of the laundry. She insisted that real life was passing her by. Well, there are probably thousands of women who would gladly exchange places with her. This young mother had all the elements for domestic happiness — a better than average house, a husband who loved her and earned a very adequate salary, and four healthy, intelligent children. Nonetheless, resentment was spoiling her life. Her self-interest was greater than her love, and her desire for personal freedom was greater than her maternal sense of responsibility.

Isn't it strange that some people who apparently have the greatest reasons to be resentful are not resentful at all? Take my friend Roger Winter, for example. With the splendid body God had given him, he became an outstanding football player and was very good at other sports. Then polio struck, and in a matter of days Roger was an invalid. When I first met him, he was in a wheelchair, being lovingly cared for by his young, attractive wife. Resentment could have made a demon out of Roger Winter, but he gave it no opportunity. Resting upon the grace of God, he found a divine sufficiency that enabled him to face life and win the battle of the spirit.

But others, like King Saul, allow resentment to destroy their lives. How quickly the heart of the king filled with jealousy and resentment as he heard the women of his kingdom singing, "Saul has killed his thousands, and David his ten thousands" (1 Sam 18:7). From that moment on, he sought in every possible way to bring David to death.

Resentments are acquired easily — resentments against people, against circumstances, against one's environment, and against one's responsibilities. Watch out for them, or they will destroy you. And I mean exactly that! I have seen many a person lose out spiritually because of harbored resentments.

Resentments rise most often in hearts that are not adequately protected by the love and grace of God. Here, they thrive like weeds in an untended garden. They are often found in persons who feel unloved, unwanted, and unappreciated. Resentment invariably accompanies self-pity.

You can wreck a wonderful marriage with resentment if you aren't careful. The whole thing unravels when selfishness outbalances love. Love "does not insist on its own way" (1 Cor 13:5), but selfishness does; love "is not irritable or resentful," but selfishness is.

There are handicaps to every job, disagreeable tasks in every life. But aren't saints people who face all the trials, endure all the heartaches, go through all the strain and struggle of life, yet maintain the attitude of Christ?

8. Are You Harboring an Unforgiving Attitude?

To be Christians, we must have the spirit of Christ abiding in our hearts; and if we have the spirit of Christ, we will forgive people even as he forgave them. Again and again Jesus emphasized the importance of the forgiving mood and the danger of holding an unforgiving attitude. When asked how many times one should forgive a person who has offended us, Jesus said, "Seventy-seven times" (Matt 18:22). He meant that a real Christian will forgive everybody of everything all the time, no matter what they have said or done. I think it significant that it was right after Jesus had taught his disciples the Lord's Prayer that he said, "For if you forgive others their trespasses, your heavenly Father will also forgive you; *but if you do not forgive others, neither will your Father forgive your trespasses*" (Matt 6:14–15, emphasis added).

I know a woman who will not forgive her sister. She has a monumental grudge against her, and this has been going on for years. We visited her one time, hoping to lead her to Christ and a transforming experience of divine love. She was moved as we talked with her, and I thought she was about to surrender. Then someone said, "Of course, if the Lord forgives you, you'll be glad to forgive your sister, won't you?"

At this she stiffened and said, "If becoming a Christian means I have to forgive my sister, I'll die and go to hell first." It was a shocking and foolish thing to say, but during the ensuing years, she has never, to my knowledge, changed her mind. How foolish — and how dangerous! This woman has carried a continual burden of sickness and pain. She alienated and finally lost her husband. Her whole life could be transformed if she would only forgive.

An unforgiving attitude festers in the dark and shadowy places of the soul. In fact, your first indication that something is wrong may be an awareness of growing anxiety. You say to yourself, "What's the matter with me?" Why do I feel this way? You begin tracing the source of your anxiety until you come to the realization that you began feeling this way the day your boss's nephew got a promotion you were sure you were in line for. This apparent injustice triggered a spark, which became a small flame and then a larger flame. This is exactly the way it works.

Perhaps a teenage son or daughter whom you brought up "in the discipline and instruction of the Lord" (Eph 6:4) decided to ignore your training and went afoul of the law or drifted into moral difficulty. You had to ask your pastor to appear with you and your teenager in juvenile court. How humiliating and discouraging!

In such a case, it is very easy to pick up an unforgiving attitude toward your own children. If you aren't careful, you may find yourself criticizing other parents and their children, saying, "If the truth were known, their kids are probably worse than mine. They just haven't been found out."

Do you see how necessary it is to have an overflow of godly love in our hearts at all times, for everybody?

Sometimes our first need is to find a warmly forgiving attitude toward God, against whom we have been holding a private grudge—ever since the baby died, ever since that drunk smashed our car and us with it, ever since that time we prayed and nothing happened.

Some time ago, I counseled with an elderly woman in a Western city who said, "I don't think God should have taken my husband away from me. I needed him." When asked how old he was when he died, she replied, "Seventy-two."

"And how long had you been married?"

"Fifty years."

"Was he a Christian?"

She answered, "The finest man I ever knew." But she felt that God should not have let him die.

I finally said, "Sister, I think you should change your attitude toward the Lord, and toward your husband's death. Every day you ought to thank God for the privilege of living with a fine Christian man for half a century. You ought to thank him for the hope of being with your husband again, very shortly, in that land beyond the sunset."

But she would not. She had picked up an unforgiving attitude toward God, and she held onto it.

Whenever we do this, we need to change. We need to pray until our unforgiving attitude turns into one of heartfelt forgiveness. God has never wronged us. He has never done anything for which he needs to ask our forgiveness. We ought to love God so honestly and sincerely that we will never have anything but the most trusting attitude toward him.

Examine your heart carefully. Do you harbor an unforgiving attitude toward anyone — even toward God?

---

9. Have You Forgiven Everyone?

Some people need to forgive their parents, particularly if parental harshness or overindulgence gave a twist to their personalities as children. How often this has happened. If you want to give your child a bad start in life, be a heavy-handed, harsh, domineering parent — or, on the other extreme, be a parent who has the mistaken idea that love means giving a child everything he wants. Either way, your child will grow up with a debilitating sense of insecurity, unable to make sound decisions. I've counseled with many such youth after they were in college.

A few years ago, I was beginning a series of sermons on the Lord's Prayer and my first message was based on the words "Our Father." Following the benediction, a young college student asked for a private conversation with me. In my study, he said, "You know, Pastor, when you said the word *Father*, it made me angry because it made me think of my own father, and he was the meanest man I ever knew. I can't remember a day in my life while I was still living at home that he didn't whip me. Most of those whippings I didn't deserve. He whipped me until I was big enough to run away and escape. I think he would have killed me had he caught me then. I can never forget his unreasonable cruelty. Pastor, do you think I can ever forgive my father?"

A young college girl came to occupy that same chair and poured out her heart. After she was seated, she continued sobbing as if her heart would break. It was some time before she could control her emotions enough to speak. Then she said, "I heard your sermon on 'Our Father.' But what an awful, wicked man my father is!" She broke down again as sobs shook her body. Then in her anguish, she poured out a heartrending story of repeated criminal violations of her person on the part of her father. She said, "I feel so dirty, so wicked, so impure. I've hated that man as I have never hated another person on earth. A hundred times I have wanted to kill him. I would have shot him or plunged a butcher knife into him had it not been for the fact that his death would have left my mother and the younger children without any means of support. Pastor, do you think I can ever forgive my father?"

I assured her, as I had assured the young man before her, that the Lord would pour his holy love into her heart until she would not only be able to forgive her father but find a genuine burden for him so that she could honestly pray for his conversion. And I am sure that is exactly what happened.

If necessary, forgive your parents and learn to love them. Then try to live so close to the fountainhead of love and grace that you will not hand on to your children the bad treatment or bad attitudes with which your own parents handicapped you.

You also need to forgive yourself. This may not at first strike you as being very important, but believe me when I say that it is of the greatest importance. The chief spiritual difficulty for many Christians today lies in the fact that they have never forgiven themselves for the sinful things they did before they gave their hearts to God.

During the years I was speaker on the *Christian Brotherhood Hour*, I received thousands of letters from people who were in trouble or had problems about which they needed counsel. One particular kind of letter I learned to recognize after reading the first few lines, because they followed a similar pattern. Each one would begin something like this:

For many years, I have listened to your broadcast and you have helped me often. I felt I ought to write to you of my appreciation. I am forty-five years old and married to a wonderful man, a fine Christian. He is chairman of the board of trustees at our church. We have three lovely teenagers, and all are living for the Lord and active in the youth organization at the church. I have been a Christian for twenty-five years.

But something is wrong. I don't know the joy that should be the experience of every Christian. Prayer isn't meaningful to me, and I read the Bible only out of a sense of duty. Church services don't bring to me the inspiration that others draw from them. What do you think is wrong with me?

My reply would be on this order:

My dear friend: Thanks so much for sharing your problem. I hope to be of some help to you, and am almost sure I have a key to the solution of your difficulty. But first, I need another letter from you. Since you have trusted me this far, may I suggest that you go ahead and pour out your heart in confession? I feel there is something you need to have lifted from your heart.

Invariably, the second letter would come back, and indeed it would be a letter of confession. Perhaps the writer had been guilty (as were most of us) of doing some foolish thing during the high school years. Or perhaps, shortly after marriage, with her husband off to war, she had surrendered to the importunities of a handsome, sensual man and had done something that she would regret to her dying day. How she hated herself! She had honestly and sincerely repented of the whole thing, and God had forgiven her. She had confessed to her husband. He too had graciously forgiven her and had never mentioned the matter since. But for some reason, the forgiveness of God and her husband did not bring back the former joys of salvation, and she could not understand why. So I would write back to remind her that although she had been forgiven by God and by her husband, she had never forgiven herself.

I shared this during a sermon in Michigan one evening, and after the service, a woman of perhaps sixty-five took my hand warmly in both of hers and said, "Thank you, Brother Oldham, for what you did for me this evening!"

I said, "Would you like to tell me about it?"

She replied, "Well, briefly, I was the woman you were talking about in your sermon tonight. I had exactly that same experience. Forty-five years ago, I did something that I will always regret, and afterward I was heartbroken because of it. I couldn't forgive myself.

"Oh, I went to the Lord right away in genuine repentance, and he was good enough to forgive me. But I've always felt soiled. I've always felt that I was totally unworthy and no good. But tonight, after being bound like that for forty-five years, I was set free. Thank you, Brother Oldham, for I will be free the rest of my life. Although the Lord forgave me away back there, I have never been willing to accept any responsibility in the work of the church.

"You see, whenever I was asked to accept some responsibility, I'd say to myself, 'You mustn't do it. It would be sacrilege. You aren't good enough to work side-by-side with those wonderful Christian people.' So Satan, through his accusations, robbed the church of forty-five years of my services. But now, thank God, I'm free."

As she told her story, I thought of Jesus' words, "You will know the truth, and the truth will make you free" (John 8:32).

I've said three things about forgiveness in these two chapters: First, forgive God if you hold an unforgiving attitude toward him. Second, forgive your parents if they mistreated or misguided you. And third, forgive yourself, lest you rob God of your service. In fact, we need to forgive everybody of everything. Remember the text quoted earlier, "If you forgive others their trespasses, your heavenly Father will also forgive you; but if you do not forgive others, neither will your Father forgive your trespasses" (Matt 6:14–15).

Forgive, my Christian friend! Give the matter up to God, and then forget it. You'll feel that you have just been given a new lease on life.

10. Love: The Key to a Christian Personality

The greatest tragedy of the human spirit is for us to live without love; and some people seem incapable of loving. But the person who does not love is out of tune with God and his universe.

I came across a very meaningful sentence in a book by Dr. David Abrahamsen. He wrote, "Our capacity to love in an adult way…is therefore equivalent only to our emotional maturity."[2] Think about that. If our emotions are out of control, we cannot love in a mature way.

This is why it is generally dangerous to marry at sixteen, for to be an adolescent emotionally is to be an adolescent in our relationships with other people, in our ability to love and receive love. Sixteen-year-olds may plead with their parents for permis-

---

2. David Abrahamsen, *The Road to Emotional Maturity* (Englewood Cliffs, NJ: Prentice-Hall, 1958), 252–53.

sion to marry, emphasizing again and again how much they love each other. And they do love each other, as much as they are capable of loving. But emotional immaturity is there, and if they are given permission to marry, the honeymoon may be over in thirty days. Only as a person becomes emotionally mature and stable can love be meaningfully expressed.

The amazing thing is that when you love God — really love God in a mature, adult manner — you will find yourself able to love everyone on the face of the earth. No, don't dismiss that statement, for it is true. When you love God with all your heart, love becomes more than something you do; it becomes a quality of your life. You not only love, you are love. Love emanates from your very soul. It reaches out to touch everyone and everything around you.

This is why it's sad to see people who seem to think that love is in limited supply, that we can genuinely love only one or two persons. I once knew a widowed mother whose only son was the center of her universe. As he grew toward manhood, she thought more and more of how cozy it would be if this handsome, charming boy would reject marriage so that he might give all of his time and attention to her. While yet in high school, her boy would occasionally bring a girl home and say, "Mother, I want you to meet Mary." His mother would say the proper things, smile, and be courteous; but later on, when her son would ask, "Well, Mother, how did you like Mary?" she would reply, "Oh, I thought she was a lovely child, very pretty. Intelligent, too. But..." Then she would glibly proceed to butt Mary right out of the picture by pointing out some minor fault or imperfection.

The mother did this with every girl her son introduced, but the lad eventually saw through his mother's conniving. In his early twenties, he brought home another girl, introduced her, and then floored his mother by saying, "We are going to be married in June."

His mother was shocked, hurt, and pained. She wept. She became physically ill. She did everything within her power to draw sympathy to herself. But her son went ahead and married the girl, and they lived happily together for more than forty years. The poor widowed mother didn't seem to realize that her son could love his wife as a wife ought to be loved and still love his mother as a mother wishes to be loved. But a mature Christian finds there is enough love to go around.

A healthy love for others begins with understanding yourself, being able to accept and respect yourself. If you do not like yourself or if you do not have confidence in your own moral integrity, you are going to have difficulty with other people. No person can despise himself without this creeping into all his social relationships. What we think of ourselves eventually becomes evident in what we think of people and how we treat them. A great deal of our irritation with people stems from irritation with ourselves. Respect for others is based on respect for ourselves.

Five years ago, a couple stood before the minister of their church and was joined together in holy matrimony. They now have two lovely children. But during the past several months, this husband has been having a clandestine affair with another woman. He knows better, for he was raised according to Christian standards, so this has brought a heavy burden of guilt to his heart. He hates himself for the way he has violated his conscience and sinned against his wife. He is late coming in one evening and his wife casually asks where he has been. He flies into a rage, tells her to mind her own business, and declares that he will come and go as he pleases. His unwarranted response triggers his wife's anger and starts an argument. Finally, in frustration, he slaps her—a terrible thing to do.

When you lose self-respect, you lose respect for others as well.

On the other hand, you can actually "love your neighbor as yourself" (Matt 19:19), and it is impossible for you to love him more than that. When you know God's full and free forgiveness, when your soul is shut up and secretive no more, but open and clear, then you are able to accept the love of God and your soul will be liberated in him. Then you are free to love in a wonderful, Christian way; and as you begin to love, others will begin to love you. How marvelously our personalities change when we open our hearts wide to God's love.

The selfish, domineering person, who rides roughshod over his family, his friends, or his employees, certainly is not free. He is bound in a prison of his own making and is very unhappy. His very possessiveness is an open indication of his lack of love and of a deep-seated insecurity. I know, for I was once a domineering person.

I have changed, I am sure, since that revelation some years ago; but nothing ever shook me as did the realization that I was a domineering person. What a shock for a man who had been for years telling other people how to live! In my agony of spirit, I began to search for the cause and a cure.

I found several reasons why persons become domineering. However, I found one thing was consistent: the domineering person is always lacking in love. His domineering disposition is an indictment at this point.

If you love a person, you will not try to possess him or bend him forever to your will. True love never enslaves; it always liberates. In a relationship of love, you put yourself in the other person's place. There is empathy between you. You are partners — bound together, yet free. True love attunes your whole personality with that of another, and it is the most rewarding and satisfying relationship that anyone can know.

Remember, the quality of our relationship with God is nowhere more apparent than in the quality of our love.

11. Does the Holy Spirit Abide Within?

The Bible tells us to live by the Spirit, walk in the Spirit, be led by the Spirit, mind the things of the Spirit, pray in the Spirit, and sing in the Spirit. This being the case, you would expect spirituality to be the chief characteristic of the people of God, because the New Testament church is a spiritual house made up of spiritual people. But there can be no genuine spirituality unless the Spirit of God dwells within us.

Are you filled with the Spirit? Do you demonstrate the presence and power of the Spirit in your daily life? In my mail and personal conversations, the question has come up again and again: "How can I know whether or not the Holy Spirit lives within me?"

There are certain dependable indications of his indwelling presence. The first is love—love for God, love for the church, love for the lost, love for everybody. This is the chief characteristic of the Spirit-filled life.

Grouchiness, peevishness, irritability, inability to get along with people—aren't these the result of a lack of perfected love in the heart? Shouldn't they be corrected through the operation of the Holy Spirit as our love increases? It is when "our hearts do not condemn us" (1 John 3:21) that we are able to love in such fashion. It is when we have a deep love for God and the things of God that true spiritual power is given. Love is like a golden cord running through all discussion of Christian spirituality.

The second manifestation of the Spirit's indwelling presence is power. "You will receive power when the Holy Spirit has come upon you" (Acts 1:8). What is involved in this power? For one thing, it means you are able to put first things first and keep them there. Spiritual power causes a person to seek first the kingdom of God and his righteousness. It means you are able to control your tongue. You don't stand there, red in the face, telling someone off if the Holy Spirit controls your life. Love doesn't act that way. It also means the power to control your desires, particularly as this applies to money matters.

I heard of a man whose monthly debt payments totaled five dollars a month more than his income. He couldn't control his desires, bought beyond his ability to pay, and was in deep trouble because of this weakness in his personality. His wife was angry because she could have no new clothes. The man had not a penny for the church, and that brought him under condemnation. Then, to justify himself, he began to criticize the church and the pastor. But his real trouble was that he loved things more than he loved Christ and the church.

When the Holy Spirit controls our impulses, we will have a steadiness and dependability that otherwise would be absent. How many talented, capable people never accept responsibility in the church simply because they are not willing to be inconvenienced? They serve and give spasmodically. They are not seeking first the kingdom of God, but the kingdom of self. When the Holy Spirit comes into their hearts, they will find a quality of love for God and for other people, which will change all this.

The presence of the Holy Spirit gives life and meaning to worship, to prayer, and to the reading of the Word. How many people have complained to me that prayer is a meaningless exercise! But isn't prayer actually conversation with God? How can one say this is meaningless? What about being bored with Bible reading? The Bible is like a letter from the Lord. With enthusiasm, the Spirit-filled Christian will take up the Bible to eagerly seek out the ways and will of God for his life.

Let's sum this up with a short examination to see whether the Holy Spirit is abiding within our hearts. First, how are you getting along with people—members of your family, people in the church, your neighbors, your pastor, those with whom you work? Are you allowing damaging resentments to build up? Have you been showing a spirit of retaliation anywhere? Did you enjoy voting against somebody in the last church election? Are you smarting under a lack of appreciation?

A girl came to me one day to say, "Pastor, I am giving up my Sunday school class. I've been teaching these kids for three years. In all that time, not one parent has ever come to say he appreciated what I was doing for his child. I'm quitting."

To her surprise, I answered, "I think you ought to."

She looked as if I had slapped her. I explained, "Well, if you are teaching for the appreciation of those parents, you may as well quit, because you aren't going to get much of it. If you are teaching in order to tell boys and girls of the love of God, of the difference between right and wrong, of the redemption Christ makes available to them, then I think you will want to go on with your class." She kept the class, and I was glad.

Do you feel that people are forever imposing on you? Are you always making a bid for sympathy? All these things are indications of spiritual immaturity and should come to correction when the Holy Spirit comes in to baptize you with holy love.

The Holy Spirit is the spirit of love, kindness, forgiveness, and longsuffering. His coming will liberate you from the bondage of self, quicken your spiritual imagination, sensitize you to human needs, and fit you into the body of Christ, which is the church. How desperately we need this divine infilling!

Have you received the Holy Spirit since you believed?

12. Is Meekness Weakness?

I attended a meeting where one woman apparently thought she was born to command. She was issuing orders right and left—not making suggestions, but telling people what to do—although they were simply her neighbors, friends, and relatives. Perhaps subconsciously, she was seeking to bring every one of them under her control. As indicated in a previous chapter, such a domineering attitude is completely foreign to the spirit of holy love. It may appear that such assertive, commandeering persons rule the earth, but the words of Jesus keep burning through: "Blessed are the meek, for they will inherit the earth" (Matt 5:5).

Meekness is a strange word in times like these, when swaggering national leaders threaten to fight each other. But Jesus said that the meek, not the swaggering warmongers, will finally be triumphant.

What is meekness? The meekness Jesus mentioned is the grace and power to wait, the ability to relax and trust the future into the hands of God. Meekness is never self-assertive; yet it has staying power. As the reformer Theodore Beza told a royal envoy, "The church is an anvil upon which many hammers have been broken." Thousands of sneering people have discounted its power; yet after looking back over the pages of history, the verdict is that Jesus was right and the advocates of hatred and force were wrong. They are still wrong.

In the 1920s, Charles Rann Kennedy wrote a play, titled *The Terrible Meek*, built around the crucifixion of Jesus. It is a conversation between a Roman centurion and Mary, the mother of Jesus. The centurion says to Mary, "We go on building our kingdoms—the kingdoms of this world. We stretch out our hands, greedy, grasping, tyrannical, to possess the earth. Domination, power, glory, money, merchandise, luxury, these are the things we aim at; but what we really gain is pest and famine…dead and death-breathing ghosts that haunt our lives forever…Possess the earth? We have lost it. We never did possess it. We have lost both earth and ourselves in trying to possess it."[3]

What does meekness have to do with a warring, threatening age like ours? Did any army recruiting poster ever advertise for meek soldiers? Did you ever know a marine sergeant to ask for the "poor in spirit" to volunteer? No, military leaders look for proud, arrogant soldiers, soldiers who are not too worried about the effects of violence upon others or upon their own consciences. They don't want volunteers who will turn the other cheek or go the second mile, for in their delusion they think that meekness is weakness. But they are wrong — dead wrong — for the "terrible meek" will outlast them all.

---

3. Charles Rann Kennedy, *The Terrible Meek*. Quoted in Sherwood Eliot Wirt, *The Cross on the Mountain* (New York: Thomas Y. Crowell Company, 1959), 42.

Remember Adolph Hitler? He and his cronies poked fun at Christianity, ridiculing the church and such old-fashioned virtues as honesty, reverence, humility, and meekness. As many of our contemporaries are doing, they laughed at morality and decency; they scorned people of sensitive conscience. But isn't it strange that Hitler found the church to be the only organization in Germany he could not conquer?

Webster defines meekness as "mildness of temper; gentle; not easily provoked or irritated; given to forbearance under injuries." *Meekness* stems from a Greek word meaning "mild and gentle." Bible commentator Adam Clarke said that the only English word which comes close to expressing the original meaning of the term is *gentleman*. A gentleman is considerate of others, thoughtful of their needs, and polite. He never insists on having his own way. He never takes the best for himself when a choice must be made between him and his brother. You never see him elbowing people out of the way. Instead, he extends to everyone else the liberties that are his by right. He is never selfish, for how could he be selfish and meek at the same time?

A gentleman has an amiable temper. You don't have to elect him chairman in order to insure his cooperation. He doesn't swagger, boast, or try to impress you with his importance. He is never vulgar in the handling of his money, even if he happens to control a great deal of it. You never hear him boasting of his goodness, his generosity, or of how much he has suffered and sacrificed for "the cause."

Someone has said that meekness is self-control under pressure. It is the ability to love and pray for someone who slanders you or lies about you. It is the ability to keep your head when others have lost theirs—and are blaming the results on you! It is the ability to hold your tongue when someone lashes out at you in uncontrolled anger, jealousy, or frustration. Meekness is bold as a lion where principles are involved, but it can also be tender as a baby's smile. We might paraphrase Jesus' words: "Blessed are those who control themselves, for they shall inherit the earth."

In his classic novel *The Robe*, Lloyd Douglas imagines a conversation between a young woman and the sick Emperor Tiberius. They are speaking about the new Christian movement. With weak voice, Tiberius says, "Diana, it might be interesting to watch this strange thing develop. If it could go on the way it seems to be going now, nothing could stop it. But it won't go on that way. It will collapse after awhile. Soon as it gets in a strong position. Soon as it gets strong enough to dictate terms. Then it will squabble over its offices and spoils. The Christian afoot is a formidable fellow… but…a Christian on horseback will be just like any other man on horseback. This Jesus army will have to travel on foot…if it expects to accomplish anything."[4]

---

4. Lloyd C. Douglas, *The Robe* (Boston: Houghton Mifflin Company, 1943).

Tiberius, you were right. Only the meek inherit the earth.

Blessed are those who love when others hate, who build when others destroy, who forgive when others remain full of malice, who dare to be real Christians when surrounded by those who take upon themselves Christ's holy name but live devoid of his spirit. How can we grow spiritually without this spirit of meekness in control of our lives?

---

13. So You Want to Belong

One man said to me, "I feel like an outsider in my own family. I just don't belong." Another spoke similarly of the coffee-break group where he works. You know how it is: You get a cup of coffee and perhaps a doughnut, and then join a little conversation group for ten minutes of chatter and relaxation.

This fellow said, "I'm not one of them. Whenever I edge up toward the group, they all clam up, and the silence lets me know I'm not welcome." It made him feel like a social outcast.

Why do people feel like outsiders when they want to be accepted by a group? Well, if you feel that way, maybe you *are* different. The nondrinker invariably feels out of place among company officers who never hold an executive meeting without serving a round of drinks. A clean-minded Christian man strolls up to a group while an off-color story is being told and they don't feel comfortable, so they walk away from him. The person with high principles invariably gets the brush-off from people who are willing to compromise their ethical standards.

However, millions want to be liked without bothering to be likable, so people keep them at arm's length. Often the person thus shut out becomes a problem to society. The rejected person wants to strike back, to get even. Inside, something is saying, "I'll show 'em!"

Psychologists tell us that self-centeredness is responsible for much of this. When our self-interest is overwhelmingly greater than our interest in other people, loneliness is inevitable. The sense of belonging has a certain price tag attached to it: the price of sharing, cooperating, and participating in group activities and projects.

For example, you don't have to support the United Way in your community, but if your coworkers discover that you are a holdout, you may be criticized. If they have pledged some of their own hard-earned money to support community needs, they may resent it if you ride free. If a neighbor's house is burning, you don't have to help carry out the furniture, but your refusal may later become a subject of conversation.

If you want to belong, you must accept your share of responsibility in the group. Community life is never really free. "Give, and it will be given to you" (Luke 6:38). Hold out, and people will hold out on you.

Again and again, I must come back to the importance of love in discussing our mutual problems. How important it is! But many of us fail at this point. A person may attend a certain church for years and then say, "I don't feel that I'm one of them. I don't feel at home there." Closer examination usually reveals this person isn't investing enough time, money, and energy there. The church "outcast" is usually holding out somewhere. You've got to be a "stockholder" in order to have a genuine stake in the life of your church.

If you want to belong to a local congregation of Christians, you must become one with them in spirit, purpose, activity, and responsibility. Share their dreams, their worship, their work, their giving for local and worldwide needs. Be willing to share in any persecution they may draw because of their spirit and work. Never utter a word of destructive criticism against a single member. (Nothing breaks fellowship more quickly than criticism, secret or open.) And when the people of your church stick out their necks on a moral issue in the community, stick your neck out also.

We reap as we sow. When we love, we are loved in return. When we hate, we are eventually hated. If we are critical, we are criticized. If we show hostility or distrust, it is given back to us.

How much do you really want to belong with other Christians? Are you willing to pay the price?

---

14. Do You Have to Be First?

Why should we be embarrassed or discouraged if we find ourselves on the "second team"? Many people have found greatness on the "second team" but lost it when they insisted on being first. It would appear that some of us are molded by nature to occupy supporting roles in the drama of life.

I remember a young man who made an excellent showing as assistant to the manager of a large store. Given a list of duties, he faithfully performed every task well and expeditiously. In fact, he was so good that the owner urged him to accept the manager's job, so he moved into top place. Within six months, he suffered a nervous breakdown. Supporting the manager, he was great; but as manager, he quickly worried himself into illness. Moved back again to the job of assistant, he recovered his health and again sparkled in the niche where he fit best.

Isn't it true that our talents, training, personality, and intelligence often determine the kind and amount of responsibilities we can handle? Sometimes a shipping clerk can rise to become president of the company, but other shipping clerks may have to remain just that, in which case they should determine to be the best shipping clerks possible.

Both types of workers are needed in every business. Some people were born to be first-class secretaries, and business could not be carried on without them. On an airplane, the navigator is as important as the pilot. A church must have not only a pastor but teachers, singers, trustees, clerks, ushers, a custodian, and givers. All are important. So instead of being impatient over the station in life where our talents have landed us, shouldn't we decide to do our best with what we have, right where we are?

Andrew, one of Christ's faithful disciples, was often referred to as Simon Peter's brother. Do you think this irked him? I doubt it. An elderly minister said the other day, "I enjoy substituting for the pastors around me when they must be absent from their pulpits." I asked a factory worker recently about his job. He said, "I was hired just to take the place of people who are off sick or on vacation. So I have to be able to handle every job in the shop." He was a substitute, a good one, and proud of it.

Well, don't we need substitutes? Doesn't somebody have to occupy second place?

Years ago, I had to come to terms in a very realistic way with my own limitations. In many ways, I realized, nature had fitted me for second place. I could sing, but not as well as many of my friends. I could speak, but others were far more effective on the platform. I was an athlete of fair ability, but I was invariably beaten in the semifinals.

In the local YMCA, where I had played tournament handball for years, I was asked to instruct a class of beginners in the game. One young, slender redhead showed exceptional promise and learned quickly, so I gave him special attention. Within two years, he could beat his teacher at the game. In a few more years, he became state singles champion.

I couldn't become a champion, but I trained one. He got the medal, and I helped prepare him for it. This experience taught me that every drama of life has supporting roles. We are not bound to be first; we are only bound to be faithful and true. You may not have ten talents, or even five, but you can invest the one or two you do have so conscientiously that at the last day the Lord will say, "Well done, good and trustworthy slave;...enter into the joy of your master" (Matt 25:23).

---

15. When Life Goes Stale

D o you awake in the morning with no feeling of expectancy? A troubled man once said to me, "I hate to open my eyes in the morning and know I am at the beginning of another uninteresting, meaningless day." I hope you never feel like that; yet many do.

Boredom can lead to disaster. A prominent psychologist has said, "While boredom is not immediately a destructive emotion, it leads directly to, and therefore is responsible for, more illness, more disruption of living, and even crime, than is caused by any single condition of the spirit."

Why are people bored in such an interesting world as this? Boredom is often the result of a failure to use our God-given imagination in a wholesome and creative way.

Take marriage, for example. Many married couples have been bored with each other ever since they returned from their honeymoon. They started out together in an interesting partnership, but the glamour soon wore off and life settled down to a monotonous routine, devoid of freshness and excitement. Marriage should never become a stale experience, but some folks seem totally unaware that it calls for constant adjustment to life and to each other.

My wife gave me more than a subtle hint in this direction one time, and I will never forget it. As pastor of Park Place Church, my work was unending and the days were long. There were always meetings and counseling and sermon preparation. There were sick people to visit and community affairs that must not be neglected. One day, my wife found my date book lying on the dresser and an idea came to her. She opened it week by week to the pages stretching ahead in the next three months, and on every space representing Monday nights, wrote, "No dates please." I appreciated it. We'd be in a gathering and someone would suggest that the board or committee should meet the next Monday night at 7:30. I'd look at my date book and say, "Sorry, I have a previous appointment." It was a private joke for Polly and me, but it did a lot for our marriage. If you are a minister's wife, why don't you try it?

All husbands need to remember that a neglected wife is an unsatisfied wife. I didn't say dissatisfied, but unsatisfied. She becomes bored, and unhappiness invariably follows.

I well remember a ministerial student who was too busy for the good of his marriage. He was in school during the morning and worked till 11:00 at night. Weekends he was off preaching somewhere, often without his wife. She was a beautiful but lonely girl, and her husband was heartbroken when she left him. But could he conscientiously place all the blame on her? People will do anything to break the monotony of a boring life — and I do mean anything.

Many people are bored with their work. I was employed for a time in a machine shop, where operations were often dull and routine. I repeated simple machine operations a seemingly endless number of times each day. The motion of the machine and the noise of the shop drove me to distraction, until I found I could escape it all through the use of creative imagination. From that time forward, although my hands were busy with my machine, my mind was meditating on the Word of God. How many times of high worship I enjoyed as I stood there! The good Lord enabled me to transmute potential boredom into refreshing streams of spiritual and mental enrichment. I learned I could fight boredom in a constructive way and win.

Put your God-given imagination to work for good. Pick up a blade of grass, a rosebud, a grain of wheat, and let your imagination loose on it. Start counting your blessings and praising God for them. Quit thinking about the things you do not have and begin thanking God for all you do have. Begin looking for every good point you can find in your neighbor. Open your eyes wide to discover some need near you that God wants you to alleviate. Somebody needs you! You can encourage the discouraged, lift someone's burden, dry someone's tears, sit by the bedside of a sick neighbor, or take someone to church with you next Sunday.

A person who engages in intercessory prayer is seldom bored. Such a prayer ministry can open a refreshing fountain for the enrichment of the soul. We can all learn the secret of the overflowing spiritual cup: It's the result of full surrender to God, giving ourselves to him for service that is motivated by love for him and the people around us.

Think about it.

---

16. How to Fight the Blues

At one time or another, all of us have suffered from a temporary depression of the spirit. Sometimes we call it discouragement or "the blues." Whatever we call it, if this feeling persists, it can defeat our hopes and plans for the future.

D. L. Moody, a great evangelist of the nineteenth century, once became very depressed because he thought the Lord was not sufficiently blessing his ministry. He was cast down and blue, and everyone around him was affected by it. He spoke disparagingly of the meetings he was holding and their poor results. He remained in this depressed condition for several months. One Monday, he met another minister who was curious to know the results of Moody's services the day before. He asked Moody, "What kind of a day did you have?"

"No good," Moody replied. "No power. I preached about Noah."

Brightening, the other preacher said, "Noah? Did you ever really study up on Noah? He was a most wonderful character."

When he got home, Moody thought perhaps he had overlooked something. So he took his Bible and again read the familiar story of Noah. The thought came to him: "Poor Noah. He preached righteousness for 120 years and never had a single convert outside of his own family."

A day or two later, Mr. Moody talked with a young preacher who had just closed a meeting in which there had been ten converts. Moody said to himself, "How happy Noah would have been with that kind of success!"

Later still, a young man said, "Mr. Moody, I want you to pray for me." Again, Moody reflected, "What Noah would have given just to hear one man say that! Just one in 120 years!" So Moody quoted to himself Psalm 42, which asks, "Why are you cast down, O my soul, and why are you disquieted within me? Hope in God" (v. 5). Moody did take hope, found victory over his discouragement, and again became a successful evangelist. But had he not learned how to overcome, his discouragement may have put him out of the ministry, just as it has ruined the lives of thousands. There is a lifting power in the reading of the Word.

Discouragement can be caused by a number of things. Sin, unrepented of, is probably the most common cause for depressed spirits. It brings not only a sense of guilt but also a feeling of separation from God.

Ill health often leads to discouragement, partly because one's physical energy is low.

In such a case, it is easy for one's natural optimism to give place to foreboding and fear. Glandular upsets sometimes bring discouragement, as does excessive fatigue over an extended period of time.

On the other hand, isn't it amazing how much trouble some people can take and still remain cheerful? An old lady in England came through one bombing after another during World War II with admirable calm and fortitude. When asked how she could be so confident, she replied, "Well, every night I say my prayers, knowing God is always watching over his own. Then I go to sleep. After all, there's no need for both of us to stay awake!"

I like that, don't you? God never forsakes his own. Just that fact should be enough to lift us out of any hour of deep discouragement.

A businessman of fifty-four was thrown out of work when his company failed, through no fault of his own. His pastor called, expecting to find him depressed, but instead the executive said, "Through all this, I think God is trying to say something to me. So I'm being quiet and listening. I'm expecting to hear from on high."

The answer was not long in coming. A few days later, the top executive of a large firm came to see him, saying, "The number four position in our company is vacant. We think you are exactly the man for the job." He was, and it was a better position than he had lost. Had he surrendered to gloom and self-pity, the offer might not have been forthcoming. Business managers want healthy-minded, optimistic people for their responsible jobs, not introspective brooders.

Don't give in to the blues! Say to yourself, "This, too, will pass! God loves me and will take care of me if I do my best for him, and keep my heart filled with faith and courage." The faith attitude is a sure cure for discouragement.

17. When You Can't Take It Any Longer

Demas was a young man who accompanied Paul on one of his missionary journeys. I imagine the youth organization of Demas's local church had a going-away party for him and presented him with a set of matched luggage. He must have been the most outstanding, talented young man in his church, and there must have been a certain amount of glamour in thus being chosen as Paul's assistant.

But the glamour soon disappeared. Demas found himself enmeshed in the hard facts of life, enduring hunger, hardship, persecution, weariness, and probably a large dose of homesickness. So he finally said, "I've had it! I'm through! I can't take it any longer. I'm going home." And back he went to Thessalonica and the marts of trade, where things would be much easier for him, at least in a financial way. (See 2 Tim 4:9–10.)

Of course, some things ought to be said in the young man's favor. Demas had become a Christian at a time when to do so was to invite trouble. He had answered a call to special service in the church. He had shown the courage to leave home and family, to launch out into a very uncertain future as the companion of an itinerant evangelist who was backed by no supporting board or society. He had deliberately gone out to live this kind of hand-to-mouth life without promise of support from any source whatsoever. So give Demas some credit. He had gone, had served, had shared the hostility and loneliness, the poverty and uncertainty.

Unfortunately for him and for the history of the church, he couldn't take it. The constant grind of life finally got him down and he lost heart and courage. It isn't hard to understand the pull of the world on Demas;

yet we always hate to see a believer give up the fight and surrender to circumstances.

Demas still lives in the experience of thousands of church people today — people who have lost heart and quit. They are defeated and down. You see, the great battles of life are fought in the heart. To maintain faith and courage, hope and optimism — to believe when others doubt and are trying to convince you of the foolishness of holding on — this is the battle. And how can we win the battle if we remove our eyes from Christ, the "pioneer and perfecter of our faith" (Heb 12:2)?

There comes a time when nobody can sustain you but God, and even he can't do it unless you trust him implicitly. The church cannot save you, no matter how glorious its history or how concerned its people.

In fact, church people may give you the greatest cause for discouragement. If you aren't careful, you will find yourself saying, "What a rotten church!" You can look at the weaknesses of other people until you forget the strength of God's "everlasting arms" (Deut 33:27 KJV). You can center your attention on a hypocrite until he assumes the size of a Goliath in your mind. You can listen to the discouragement of a vocal minority until you think that the whole church is lost. You can focus on the inconsistencies of weak, failing people until you yourself become weak and ineffective in your service to Christ.

Watch out, Christian! You're entering dangerous territory. Discouragement is a road straight to Thessalonica. The church is not going down to defeat. It is still Christ's church, and "the gates of Hades will not prevail against it" (Matt 16:18).

You may think you can't take it any longer. Can't you? Who said so? What is your real trouble? Others, or yourself? Remember, the kind of Christian you become depends on you, not on others. You can pray whether they do or not. You can live close to God, even if the whole human race is moving in the opposite direction. You can be Christlike, even if everyone around you seems to be filled with the devil. You can love and be kind when relatives and neighbors are surly, thoughtless, and unkind. You can take it! By God's grace, you can take it!

You may think you can't—can't take the spiritual sickness, the conflict, the sad reputation of your congregation; can't take the pastor or his interminable sermons; can't take his wife's personality; can't take the careless choir, the soloist, the organist, or the Sunday school teacher; can't understand the decisions of "that dumb board of trustees." Why? Is everything wrong with them but nothing wrong with you?

The fact is, you can take it! You can take poverty if you must. You can take persecution, misunderstanding, and hardship. You can say with Paul, "I can do all things through him" (Phil 4:13). But to do so, you need a liberal outpouring of God's Spirit upon your life every day. You need to get your manna fresh from him every morning. You need to stand, not in your own strength, but in the might of an omnipotent God who promised never to leave you or forsake you (Heb 13:5).

A Christian never quite reaches the breaking point. He can always hold on a bit longer!

---

18. Why Shouldn't It Happen to You?

Are you expecting the Lord to remove all thorns from every rosebush and all stones from every path? One of my radio listeners poured out a story of grief, loneliness, and heartache, then concluded, "Why should all this happen to me?" I didn't say what was on my mind, but my first impulse was to answer, "Why shouldn't it happen to you? It happened to Christ, to all the disciples, and to millions of Christians who gave their lives in martyrdom. Are you different? On what grounds would you like to claim exemption?"

Where did we get the idea that happiness is the normal lot of humanity, that trouble and grief are intruders? This isn't the case at all. "Human beings are born to trouble just as sparks fly upward" (Job 5:7). How can we expect happiness to be the norm when sin is so universal in our world? Heartbreaking experiences come to all of us. Few human beings arrive at the age of fifty without experiencing cruel grief or the blasting of some cherished dream. Jesus said to his disciples, "In the world you face persecution" (John 16:33). Then he added, "But take courage; I have conquered the world!" Tribulation is inevitable, even for Christians, but believers have the power to deal with the sternest need.

Cancer is on the increase and may appear in my body at any time. Heart disease is taking an alarming number of lives. I drive thousands of miles a year and do a considerable amount of flying. Will a drunken driver cripple or kill me some day? Will my name be posted on a casualty list following a plane crash? Only God knows the answers.

The Bible says, "It is appointed for mortals to die once" (Heb 9:27), so some day I am going to die. How or when, I do not know. What attitude should I take toward this event? Well, this is the way I face it: I place my life wholly in the hands of God.

I say with Jesus on the cross, "Father, into your hands I commend my spirit" (Luke 23:46). I am no longer my own, but his. I am his servant, and I know beyond all shadow of doubt that he loves me. I have the promise, "I will never leave you or forsake you" (Heb 13:5). Into whatever land I journey, my Lord will go before me. Whatever I face, he will be there. Whatever comes, there will be enough grace to sustain me.

Certainly, Christ knows and sympathizes with the lonely isolation of those who are in trouble, those desperately ill or face to face with death. Hasn't he already taken "the loneliest journey"? He knows what the road is like, how deep the river at the crossing, and he whispers, "Because I live, you also will live" (John 14:19).

Again, why shouldn't trouble happen to me? It happened to Paul, and he was probably the most outstanding Christian of the first century. He knew in advance that he was going to die; yet when the moment came, he went into eternity without complaint, facing the ordeal like a brave soldier and saying, "I have fought the good fight, I have finished the race, I have kept the faith. From now on there is reserved for me the crown of righteousness" (2 Tim 4:7–8).

The most important thing in life is not what happens to you, but how you take and use it. Centuries ago, a Christian martyr was being burned to death on a heated grill. When he had been thus tortured for some time, he said to his tormentors, "Would you like to turn me over? This side is done." He was in possession of his soul, and his soul was in possession of a quality of grace that lifted him completely above what his tormentors were doing to him. Paul said, "We also boast in our sufferings" (Rom 5:3). Do you? It isn't easy, but it is better to glory than to shed tears of self-pity or to "curse God and die" (Job 2:9).

The noblest saints have been put to death in gas chambers. Godly people have been stripped of their possessions and boycotted through false accusations. Why shouldn't it happen to you? or me?

Those who follow Christ for loaves and fishes will fall by the wayside when the food runs out, just as they did when Jesus walked the earth. We are not hirelings, bartering with God and promising so much service for so much grace or so much protection. We are the sons and daughters of God, heirs of the royal blood. Even though this divine nobility is in our veins, the time will come when we will suffer as others have suffered and endure the trials and tribulations common to Christians before us. Yet in Christ there is strength for each day, power to endure, courage to be true, and even "dying grace."

So dare to be true to the Lord. Dare to be obedient. And when you are at last called upon to die, let it not be with whimpering and complaining. Die like a saint! Die in the faith! Die in triumph, holding tightly and serenely to God's unchanging hand. Why shouldn't it happen to you?

---

19. How to Handle Anxiety

This is a tough world. There is a great deal of unhappiness, trouble, and tragedy in it. But the Christian lives by faith, believing in God's love and keeping power. The Christian is sure that "things work together for good for those who love God" (Rom 8:28).[5]

---

5. Some folks misquote this passage and say that everything works for good, anyhow. But that isn't what Paul said. He said that everything works for good *for those who love God.*

A great deal of the world's trouble does not disappear if we ignore it. Sensitive persons cannot remain aloof and untroubled by the heartbreak and anguish of those around them. It breaks our hearts to see a friend recklessly throwing away virtue, morality, decency, honor, and responsibility. When you see what sin does to distort people's judgment, twist personalities, and destroy families, how can you remain uncaring? We are anxious about such folks, just as we would be anxious about a man about to be swept over a waterfall in a rowboat.

Yet we can't afford to let the world and its problems get us down. If we become the victims of unrelieved worry and apprehension, these will rob us of happiness, peace of mind, joy in the Lord, and perhaps even our physical health.

Many anxieties are of our own making. I remember a woman who had been covering up a considerable amount of guilt. Her husband was a traveling man, gone days at a time on business trips; so she formed a habit of relieving her loneliness and boredom by carrying on a clandestine affair with another man. She was just "playing around" and had no intention of leaving her husband. One day, while her lover was with her in the house, news came of the death of her husband. So the opportunity of confessing to him and making things right was lost forever. As a result, she became filled with deep anxiety.

I am not a psychiatrist, but after many years of pastoral experience, I would like to make a few suggestions about how to bring anxiety under control.

First of all, you need a clear conscience. Paul told Timothy that he could wage a good spiritual warfare by holding "faith with a clear conscience" (1 Tim 3:9). Hebrews 9:14 says that only the blood of Christ can purify the conscience and rob it of its power to condemn. When we experience God's full forgiveness through repentance and faith, the basic cause for many of our anxieties fades away. First John 3:21 says,

"If our hearts do not condemn us, we have boldness before God." And note this word in Hebrews 10:22: "Let us approach with a true heart *in full assurance of faith*, with our hearts sprinkled clean from an evil conscience" (emphasis added). When one's conscience is carrying a burden of guilt, the first step toward peace of mind is to go to God in full confession and repentance.

Second, realize that the God you trust is very great. Be mindful of his omnipotence, his ability to take care of you under every circumstance. A vital, strong, living faith in God is an absolute essential if you would know freedom from anxiety. I am reminded of the faith of my own sainted father. What a quiet, unassuming confidence he had in God! Till the day of his death, he never lost the assurance that God was with him, guiding him and taking care of him.

Third, add to your faith a genuine, warm love for God. "You shall love the Lord your God with all your heart, and with all your soul, and with all your strength, and with all your mind; and your neighbor as yourself" (Luke 10:27). Faith produces love, and love produces faith. The two intertwine and strengthen each other. The Bible says, "There is no fear in love; but perfect love casts out fear" (1 John 4:18). Since fear is the root of anxiety, love has a great deal to do with whether you have peace of mind. If you love the Lord with all your heart, you will trust him without fear.

Fourth, to combat anxiety, you need patience. When you really trust the Lord, you are able to wait for him to act. New Testament translators often used the words patience and steadfastness interchangeably. If you would do your part to be free of anxiety, let your allegiance to Christ be solid as a rock, with no reservations. "Great peace have those who love your law; nothing can make them stumble" (Ps 119:165). This is the kind of peace that conquers anxiety, the trust that cancels out fear.

Fifth, to combat anxiety, develop a strong confidence in the power of prayer.

It will change your life and sustain you in every time of need. Prayer has played a vital role in the life of every radiant, victorious Christian. How can anxieties fill you with fear after you have just given them up to God in prayer?

Next, put yourself in the presence of God by finding little islands in your day for quiet, meditation, and prayer. Don't neglect your Bible. Read especially the Psalms and Gospels, saturating your soul in the spirit of the Word, resting your heart in the promises of God.

Finally, combat anxiety with enthusiasm. Refuse to brood on your troubles. Instead, focus your mind on what is good, pure, and wholesome. Find something worth living for and give yourself to it with all your heart.

Trouble? Of course you will have trouble, but you do not stand alone against trouble. You and God can handle it together. Such a partnership is more than a match for whatever comes your way. Trust God, and be not afraid!

---

20. Faith Makes You Strong

Faith is at work in many of our ordinary activities. When you buy an automobile, you demonstrate faith in the dealer and in the thoroughness of someone's manufacturing process. A man proposes marriage to a woman, not only because he loves her, but because he has faith that she will be a good partner, wife, and mother. When you board a plane, you manifest faith in its designer and builder, faith in the navigator and pilot, faith in radio and radar operators, faith in the refiners of fuel and oil, faith in the judgment and skill of maintenance mechanics and ground crews, faith in the constancy of aerodynamics. You can't live for a single day without placing faith in someone or something.

What is faith?

Faith is a believing, trusting confidence in God, in other human beings, in things, or in ideas. Faith may move you to believe what you cannot prove, see, or touch. Faith may give you an inexplicable ability to be calm in the midst of a storm. It may give you assurance when you seem to have no basis for assurance. It may bring peace of mind. It may give you a sense of confidence about the future when at present the sky seems black as midnight.

Christian faith is confidence in God's power to bring you through your present difficulties. It works for your good and Christian growth. It is strong, stubborn, optimistic, and aggressive. Christian faith not only holds the fort but takes the offensive when you are under spiritual assault. "This is the victory that conquers the world, our faith" (1 John 5:4).

Thousands have great faith in the power of evil but little in the power of righteousness. They have more confidence in Satan's power to ruin and destroy than they have in the power of God to redeem and keep. They have more faith in the world than in the church, more confidence in the military than in the power of God to shield and protect his own. They have greater faith in the threats of the enemy than in the divine arm that is "mighty to save" (Isa 63:1).

Center your life, your plans, your ambitions, your hopes, and all in God. Be obedient to his will. Love, serve, share, trust, give, praise, pray, and adore. Live in God! Then you will find it the easiest and most natural thing to trust him and believe his promises for you. You will testify to the truth of Isaiah 40:8: "The grass withers, the flower fades; but the word of our God will stand forever." What is that word? Read verses 10–11: "See, the Lord God comes with might, and his arm rules for him...He will feed his flock like a shepherd; he will gather the lambs in his arms, and carry them in his bosom." David wrote in Psalm 37:25, "I have been young, and now am old, yet I have not seen the righteous forsaken or their children begging bread." Verse 28 adds, "For the Lord loves justice; he will not forsake his faithful ones. The righteous shall be kept safe forever."

Remember that it is good health to trust the Lord and bad health to worry, fear, and live in anxiety. Worry is a sin against your own body; it can shorten your life and embitter your personality. Worry promotes heart trouble, brings on faulty digestion, and upsets your sleep. Live the surrendered life before God, giving all your life concerns to him. He will lead you through your problems as you rest in him.

Lord Shaftsbury stood one day at a London street crossing and, while waiting for traffic to clear, saw a little girl hesitating to cross the street alone. She looked up and said, "Please, sir! Will you help me across the street?" Later, Shaftsbury said, "That little girl's confidence was the greatest compliment I ever had in my life."

I wonder if God doesn't feel complimented when you place your confidence in him and say, "Please, sir! Will you help me across?" Don't you think you can trust him?

---

22. Good Religion Means Action

Some people seem to have a delayed moment of truth when, for the first time, life becomes sharply focused so that the important and unimportant things appear in clear perspective. That moment came for Moses when he began to give serious consideration to the needs of his fellow Israelites. He had been reared apart from his people, in the house of Pharaoh. But there came a day when his superior education, economic position, and privileges dropped away, and he felt the moral necessity to help his brethren. No longer could he live in comfort while they suffered under the stinging lash of their taskmasters. No longer could he ignore the fact that he was one of them; he was not an Egyptian but one of God's chosen people. Life began for Moses only after he had come face to face with a crisis. He was no longer satisfied to be a neutral observer but instead entered the fight for justice.

How about you and me? Isn't it true that we don't really begin to live until we get out of the grandstand and on the playing field? We don't begin to live until we become participants in the battle of life.

This is a very needy world in which we live, and the chief satisfaction we will enjoy as we journey through the years will come as we exercise our prerogatives and privileges as citizens of the kingdom of God. Who can claim such citizenship and not engage in service to humanity? We serve God by serving people.

Sherman Rogers was only twenty, working in an Idaho logging camp. One day, the superintendent left for town and said, "Rogers, you are in charge while I am gone. Act like a real boss. If anyone refuses to take orders, fire him." This looked like a tailor-made opportunity to fire Tony, a glum, sour-looking Italian whom nobody liked. It was Tony's job to keep spreading sand on Hill No. 2 so that the giant log sleds wouldn't slide on the ice and run over the horses. So Rogers started toward Hill No. 2.

On the way over, Rogers encountered the owner of the operation. Sensing his mission, the owner said, "Don't bother Tony. I've been logging forty years, and Tony is the most reliable man I have ever had. He's a grouch and he hates everybody, but he stays on the job. There hasn't been an accident on his hill in the eight years he's been there, although men and horses were killed there every year before he took over."

Sherman Rogers found Tony warming a shovelful of sand over a fire. A biting wind whipped around the hill, and the temperature was well below zero. Rogers said, "Good morning, Tony. I'm the boss today. I had every intention of firing you until the owner told me what a good man you are." Then he repeated the owner's remarks word for word.

Tony was amazed. He said, "Why didn't he tell me that eight years ago?" Tears started rolling down his cheeks. That night in the bunkhouse, the men all spoke of Tony's exceptional work. One said, "That guy threw enough sand today to sand a dozen hills. And he smiled all day."

Tony insisted on taking Rogers home to meet Marie, mother of his four children. When Tony told her in Italian what had been said, she put her arms around Rogers and kissed him. Later in the evening, as Marie was putting the children to bed, Rogers heard her pray, "Dear God, help my children to grow up to be good Americans.

And try to help the American children to understand them." Rogers asked about the children. Marie explained how hard it had been for dark-skinned, poorly clothed children to bear up under the contemptuous remarks made by others, who had called them "wops," "dagos," and other disrespectful names.

The next day, Rogers went over to the school. He had the four Italian children excused from the room, then took half an hour to plead with the teacher and the other children to give Tony's youngsters a break. He asked them to treat the Italians kindly, as they would wish to be treated if they were in Italy. It was the beginning of a new day for the Italian children.

Twelve years later, Tony was superintendent of railroad construction for one of the biggest logging operations in the West when Sherman Rogers happened to see him again. Said Tony, beaming, "If it hadn't been for that one minute you talked to me back in Idaho, I'd have killed somebody by this time. That one minute changed my whole life. And that half hour you spent at school changed the lives of all four of my youngsters." He mused, "I wonder why people don't try to understand more and hate less."

Christianity means much, much more than sitting in church enjoying the organ, the hymns, and a sermon. Wholesome Christian religion will send you out to serve and bless needy people whose lives you touch from day to day. Remember, it is "the gospel according to you" that is being read by the rest of the world.

---

23. Just Across the Street

In a little book described as "non-pious meditations for ordinary people,"[6] O. H. Austin suggests that if a hotel happened to be located just right, it might

6. Orval H. Austin, *Come as You Are* (New York: Abingdon Press, 1956).

advertise thus: "Come stay with us. You'll be right across the street from everything." You can see it, can't you? A pretentious hotel situated just across the street from a huge, sprawling shopping center with dozens of businesses catering to the needs and pleasures of the people. How would you like to live "just across the street" from everything? You'd have the supermarket, the drugstore, the hardware merchant, the postal substation, the restaurant, bank, clothier, and shoe repairman all within the distance of a two-minute walk. How handy!

My mind is not on shopping centers at the moment, but on you — your life, your opportunities for improvement, and what you will do about them. It seems to me that a great many opportunities for growth, development, advancement, and service are just across the street from you. Are you taking full advantage of them?

A young man of twenty-one took a job on the maintenance staff of his state university and continued in this work until he retired at sixty-five, but he never enrolled in a single course! That is tragic. He had access to the finest of educational opportunities for nearly forty-five years but never took the slightest advantage of them. He could have kept his job and attended night classes, but he never found the ambition to do it. He lived "just across the street" from privileges that could have transformed his life, added substantially to his income, and widened the basis for personal growth. A whole new world of books could have opened up to him. It was all there, but never used. He never bothered to enroll.

A few years ago, it was my privilege to spend about a month in Japan. What a lovely country it is! How kind and friendly its people! It was so pleasant to sit in their homes, drinking tea and conversing through an interpreter, often praying with them. I enjoyed Tokyo, spread out to house its increasing millions. It was a pleasure to ride the Japanese railroads, which operate so punctually. We visited Nikko, the shrine center, and were intrigued with its ancient trees and picturesque temples. At Kamakura was the enormous and world-famous statue of Buddha. Our trip to Mount Fuji was both interesting and inspiring. So I came away from Japan grateful for the privilege of seeing its mountains and seashores, and preaching the gospel to thousands of spiritually hungry men and women.

Back in America, I met a young serviceman who had been stationed in Japan, so it was but natural to compare notes. I said, "Didn't you enjoy Yokahama and Tokyo? Wasn't Nikko interesting? Did you get out to Tachikawa?"

I was shocked by his reply. He said, "You know, I was in Japan a full year, but I never left the base where I was stationed." Just think what he missed! His weekends could have taken him to all the places I had visited and more. He was "just across the street" from a whole new world but never saw it. Faced with the privileges of a lifetime, fear or lack of curiosity robbed him of an experience for which others pay thousands. I felt sorry for him.

What is "just across the street" from you?

Isn't it true that opportunities for advancement and improvement are before all of us — all the time? Yet no one will force us to "cross the street" to take advantage of them. That is up to us.

You can find both depravity and saintliness close at hand. "Just across the street" are the bawdy houses and the churches, gambling joints and rescue missions, furtive dope peddlers and religious bookstores, burlesque theaters and concert halls. Newsstands sell pornography outside of great public libraries where one is free to examine the accumulated wisdom of the ages. "Stay with us. You'll be just across the street from everything." True! But you will decide where and to what you make the crossing.

Our greatest privilege is to make the most of our potential for God and humanity. We can grow in grace and in the knowledge of the truth. We can become better persons, day after day, as long as we live. We can delve into the Scriptures until they come alive with new beauty, radiance, and power. We can learn the secret of intercessory prayer and walk hand in hand with the Lord.

Even those who have been Christians for many years can find a wonderful new world of beauty, victory, and peace "just across the street." Too many of us are satisfied to be average Christians, but real delight comes when we seek to become exceptional servants of God. The "average Christian" standard isn't high enough. Average Christians lack power and influence. We need some saints in the church.

I want this book to help people who desire to clear away the debris that may have collected in their lives so that they can become valiant, victorious Christians. Are you, by any chance, one of them? Are you still standing on the curb, dreaming? Don't stand too long or your dreams will vanish. Cross the street to fulfill your vision. Quit merely talking about it and begin doing something to make it happen.

You have postponed excellent plans long enough. Don't waste any more of your precious time in procrastination. Procrastination can rob you of many a victory and could defeat you forever.

Is there a talent you have neglected, a potential you ought to develop? Step off the curb and begin exercising it.

Is there someone with whom you, and you alone, can effectively share the love of God? Go to that person today.

Why be an ordinary Christian when you could be an exemplary, courageous, fearless, dedicated soldier of the cross?